I Wonder Why

Baby Animals

Flip the flaps

KINGFISHER
NEW YORK

Copyright © 2008 by Kingfisher
KINGFISHER
Published in the United States by Kingfisher, an imprint of Henry Holt and Company LLC,
175 Fifth Avenue, New York, New York 10010.
First published in Great Britain by Kingfisher Publications plc,
an imprint of Macmillan's Children's Books, London.

Distributed in Canada by H. B. Fenn and Company Ltd.

Library of Congress Cataloging-in-Publication Data has been applied for.

ISBN: 978-0-7534-6220-1

Kingfisher books are available for special promotions and premiums.
For details contact: Director of Special Markets, Holtzbrinck Publishers.

First American Edition September 2008
Printed in China
10 9 8 7 6 5 4 3 2 1
1TR/0408/LFG/UNTD/140MA/C

Consultant: David Burnie

Contents

Baby animals

Thousands of baby animals are born every day. Feathery chicks and scaly lizards hatch from eggs. On hot, grassy plains, furry lion cubs and big baby elephants are born.

baby deer

mother elephant

1. Why is a baby deer spotted?

2. Where do baby animals live?

3. What does a baby elephant look like?

antlers

**baby deer with stag
(adult male deer)**

tusk

1. A baby deer has white spots to help it hide in the grass. Its father has horns on his head, called antlers.

2. Baby animals live in many different places. Some babies live in water or on ice. Other babies live in hot jungles.

3. A baby elephant looks like its mother, but it is much smaller and does not have tusks.

Where some baby animals live

Ducklings live in water.

Some baby seals live on ice.

Baby monkeys live in hot jungles.

5

Furry babies

A furry baby animal grows
inside its mother's body.
When it is born, the baby
drinks its mother's milk. The
milk helps the young animal
grow strong and healthy.

mother koala
in a tree

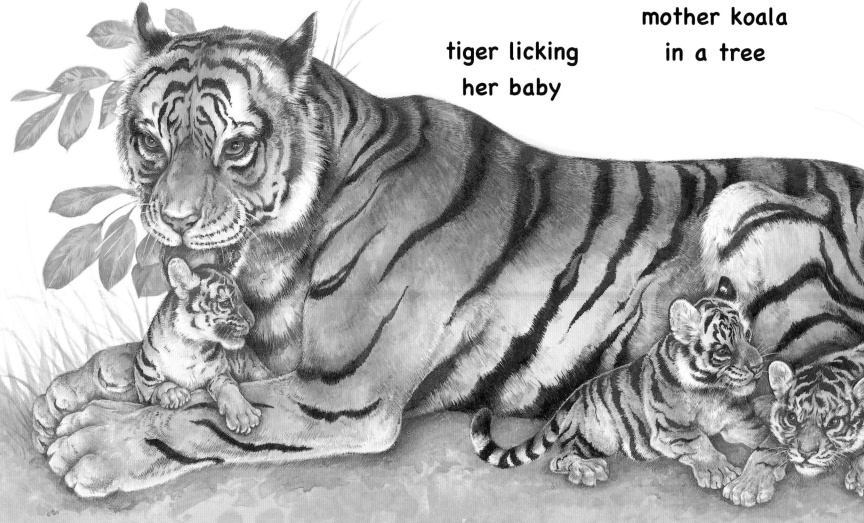

tiger licking
her baby

1. How does a koala carry her baby?

2. What do baby animals do all day?

3. Why does a tiger lick her baby?

koala baby on
mother's back

cubs drinking
mother's milk

1. A koala carries her baby on her back. The baby is too small to take care of itself.

2. Baby animals eat and sleep. Young chimpanzees also like to play.

3. A tiger licks her baby to clean its fur. A baby tiger is called a cub.

Baby chimpanzees

eating

sleeping

playing

Feathery babies

Baby birds are fluffy, but when they get older, their feathers get stronger. This helps some birds fly, such as owls, and it helps other birds swim underwater such as penguins.

Penguin chicks huddle together to stay warm.

penguin with egg on its feet

8

1. What grows inside an egg?

2. What do baby birds eat?

3. Who takes care of a baby emperor penguin?

penguin chick has hatched

1. A baby bird, called a chick, grows inside an egg. When the egg hatches, the chick comes out.

2. Most baby birds eat the food that their parents bring to the nest. Some chicks eat fruit or insects. Owl chicks, or owlets, eat mice.

3. A male penguin rests the egg on his feet. When it hatches, he keeps the chick warm under his feathers.

Owl chicks feeding

hungry owl chicks

adult owl brings a mouse

chicks eat the mouse

9

Scaly babies

Most baby reptiles, such as crocodiles and turtles, hatch from eggs. Scaly babies are often fully formed and look like tiny adults. They can take care of themselves right away.

baby chameleon

crocodile

10

1. How does a baby chameleon catch its food?

2. Where are baby turtles born?

3. What does a mother crocodile carry in her mouth?

chameleon
catching a fly

1. The baby chameleon shoots out its long, sticky tongue to catch a fly.

2. Baby turtles hatch from eggs that have been buried on a sandy beach. They then crawl to the ocean to swim away.

3. A mother crocodile carries her babies inside her mouth to keep them safe.

**crocodile babies
swimming**

Baby turtles being born

hatching from eggs

crawling

swimming

Water babies

All types of babies live in seas, ponds, and rivers. Some water babies, such as fish, can breathe underwater. Whales, dolphins, and hippopotamuses must swim up to the surface in order to breathe.

baby hippopotamus swimming

...adpole becomes a frog

1. A ba...
is bor...
in a r...

2. A ba...
to lea...
away...
up to

3. A tad...
legs ...
Finall...
and b...

1. Where is a baby hippopotamus born?

2. When does a baby hippopotamus learn how to swim?

3. How does a tadpole turn into a frog?

...oles hatch from eggs.

...en they grow legs.

...ach tadpole turns into a frog.

13

Baby homes

Some animals build nests or dig burrows for their babies. Others set up their homes in caves or tree hollows. There are also some animals that keep their babies on their bodies.

baby panda

kangaroo

14

1.

2.

3. A
co
in
un
m

joey in
a pouch

1. Where does a
baby panda live?

2. Why do baby rabbits
live underground?

3. Who pops out
of a pouch?

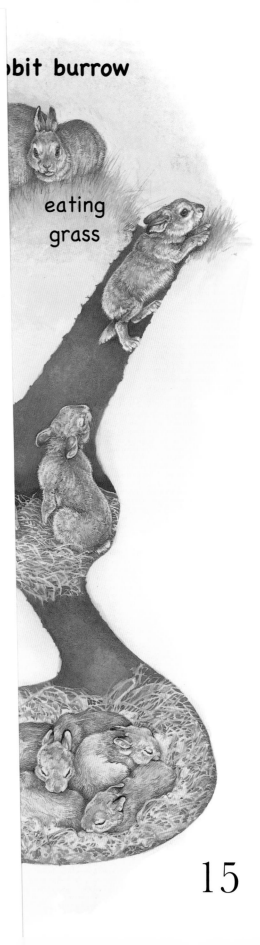

bit burrow

eating
grass

15

Growing up

Many baby animals stay with their mother or group until they are big enough to find food for themselves. They leave when they can walk, run, or fly well.

young bears play-fighting

16

1. How do baby birds
learn to fly?

2. When does a
bear grow up?

3. Why do young bears
fight with each other?

one young bear
wins the fight

1. Chicks grow long feathers and flap their wings to make them stronger. Then they try to fly from the nest.

2. A brown bear lives with its mother for three years. It becomes fully grown when it is ten years old.

3. Young bears play-fight because it makes them stronger—and it is fun!

Parrot chicks growing up

Chicks have soft feathers.

They then grow long feathers . . .

and learn to fly!

Index